PROVOCATIONS

POEMS

DAVID SCHLOSS

DOS MADRES

2023

DOS MADRES PRESS INC.
P.O. Box 294, Loveland, Ohio 45140
www.dosmadres.com   editor@dosmadres.com

Dos Madres is dedicated to the belief that the small press is essential to the vitality of contemporary literature as a carrier of the new voice, as well as the older, sometimes forgotten voices of the past. And in an ever more virtual world, to the creation of fine books pleasing to the eye and hand.

Dos Madres is named in honor of Vera Murphy and Libbie Hughes, the "Dos Madres" whose contributions have made this press possible.

Dos Madres Press, Inc. is an Ohio Not For Profit Corporation and a 501 (c) (3) qualified public charity. Contributions are tax deductible.

Executive Editor: Robert J. Murphy

Illustration & Book Design: Elizabeth H. Murphy
www.illusionstudios.net

Typeset in Adobe Garamond Pro & Out of Africa
ISBN 978-1-953252-90-6
Library of Congress Control Number: 2023943044

First Edition

ACKNOWLEDGEMENTS

Sections 2, 3 and 7 of "Dawdling" (in somewhat different form) were published as "Back Home" in *Open Letters.*

"On the Spectrum" previously appeared in *Last Stanza Poetry Journal.*

For my sister Sally

TABLE OF CONTENTS

I.

IN PASSING

II.

COSTUMES

III.
DARK MATTERS

IV.
STAGES

You never thought that you'd come home to this
old yearning— a consequence of past sins
drawn like bold tattoos all over your skin, . . .

—David Schloss, "The Messenger"

I.

IN PASSING

*"For nothing I do is like
the things I'd like to do."*

IN MY BOOK

Assiduous, I planned
to leave a living mark
upon a page, on which
I thought a mind alone
might render to myself
your face, alive beyond
a mind that wraps itself
around a loving thought
of hands that hold a line
of legs outspread in acts
of love upon some bed,
within those pages of
a book we often read
together to that end.

QUESTIONS FOR A MUSE

If I'm facing no truths I'm able and willing to tell,
do I deserve to speak of their beauty, or should I
just let things happen, as if this life were a series
made for TV, showing off my skills with nothing
to show for them but a continuous loss of belief?

Receiving the constantly unheeded urges to sing
in a sad search for meaning, what should I make
of this system in which all the prizes hang askew,
in which I never won anything before, and simply
trying seems to be my only chance of any reward?

Will it serve my purpose to find some new music
alive inside me from the little muse that feeds me
what lines I write, or will those forces of entropy
I've wished to control begin to stiffen my resolve,
with my wits caught up inside me in these nights?

BANK-ROLLING

I used to feel used up
by how I wished a world
to be, beautiful and clear.

As I was slowly going,
succumbing to a world's
immediate gratifications,

it seemed by then I was
on my own in every place
I'd have to pay for them.

With good prices offered,
I still had poor judgment
about the prices I'd pay:

I no longer want to say
what I want to do, I'd say,
but then, I'd do just that,

still on the waiting lists at
a front desk, a back room
where the names are kept.

I heard it was a good place
to place my bets. On a roll
down to bottoms of hills,

shrinking back at first, yet
closer to an end, I'm ready
to start rolling over again.

IN MY DREAMS

Are there any better facilities
to get in touch with galleries
of gargoyles, or realize as easily
how to hold my private parties
at the same times as my public
conversations, and as candidly?

Such magic's in the magic book
I've refused to refute as I come
back to my posts after tracking
my enemies, rounding them up
where the fathers and the sons
always go with their holy ghosts.

Will this sell well among savages
of fixed minds, random passions,
nightmare tales of grim slaughter;
or is it just a mercantile laughter,
as dreams seem a dime a dozen
and always, always, fluctuating?

Nothing points to *them versus us*
better than an idea about nothing
as safe without kinds of darkness
to hide in; with nothing safer than
this distance, nothing softer than
some sorts of dreaming to lie in.

We come to this world in passing,
when a world seems just a parting
from long lists of our projections
of what may come– and so I leave
the parties by the ways I've come
to see myself in what I have done.

ON MY *NOT TO DO* LIST

On my *Not To Do* list,
I make gifts to ones who,
smiling, invite me to give
gifts back to them, pained
little smirks, as grotesque
as theirs so often seem.

I'll eat whatever I'd like
with my fork and a knife;
I'm an eager eater after all,
cutting up fresh-cut meats
with my good right hand,
lifting them with my left.

I won't talk just to talk,
or even walk just to walk
away from combat zones,
trying to find a path past
these bomb-making sites
to a clearing in the light.

COMPLICATIONS OF A PARTY

As others began drinking to get drunk
in order to say what they really mean,
I would discuss just about everything,
I told them, without drinking anything:

'All the news that's fit to speak, at least,'
some sort of model precept coming out
of an open mouth in accord with moves
away from discomfort; but not quite yet.

One thing I didn't wish to mention was
how everyone there still meant to keep
saving their own attributions of success
from secrets of their usual complicities.

For hadn't I, too, elected my deceptions
with untold lusts, as all the others used
to use me for their own private purposes,
familiar faces full of what they'd refused?

*

Out of dark clouds hanging in the west,
some thunder passing over, a hard rain
cut through all the porous membranes
that we'd strung up between us by then.

I knew some people would speak of this
as though there were two sets of us there,
some other bodies telling of their truths,
disdained later as too false or debonair.

So we'd get our fifteen minutes of fame,
suffering fools, like fools after the facts
of those events, along with everyone else
under a full moon's pressure, an old pact.

I could still feel the stings of retrieving
what I knew of such acts: was anything
wrong with the assertions of one's own
blurred memory of defeats after leaving?

*

Revoking any attempts to stay in touch
with tragedies with my dry eyes closed,
it's still hard enough to think of endings
as the only alternatives we'll ever know.

So, will there be rumors, after I depart,
that I've declined, afterward, into some
deep new depression? Or is all such talk
just a case of 'false memory syndrome'?

Bravery's brevity's our companionable
companion, I think, to the lives behind
our lives, those truly deep complexities
of some other worlds we lie far beyond.

With after-images still rattling around
at the back of my mind, as if in a fever,
I'm waiting for our skins to turn silver,
but I'm still feeling as bloodied as ever.

*

For now, what almost holds these notes
towards nothingness together still serves
as new perspectives on self-preservation,
a taking of our bodies back for ourselves.

The higher the stakes the more likely are
these protestations– inviting me to fight,
framing my sentences as new rehearsals
to serve those who once 'served me right.'

Then, nothing, which I'd save, although
what I'd wanted to show, beyond my old
private calculations about how the world
really works, may never be fully exposed.

"I'm feeling much better now," I'll testify,
so, when I really feel better, I might feel
that much more likely to show how I was,
whether rightly or wrongly then, justified.

IN PASSING

Past squiggles of rubble in routes lying silent,
frozen, how hard it is to find open hydrants
in our daily searches for water, as we climb,
one hoary loner, one big fat cigar smoker,
going from town to town, two once-dutiful
anthropologists climbing up, looking down.

With nowhere else to go, but reliably primed
to lie back down inside of someone else's arms,
distorting ourselves, holding old disorders in
our skins, positing points as if under a spell
as we go, can we ever be freed to find a place
where we might be found in some other future?

Spending some time in their cities over the years,
with no more bearing up in the streets of their arms
in new protests or celebrations to the skies,
in passing, the casting of people in this light
isn't just that all former trust becomes lost when
our trips are seen just as products of what we seem.

With faces washed in light beneath impartial lamps,
shy of the effects of some reflexive reflections
inside our eyes, perhaps we'll see some peace at last:
we still want to go rock-climbing, in a wilderness
of arms, because we'd love our neighbors as ourselves,
although we've always been traveling, shyly, away.

THE POKY LITTLE PUPPY

In a trance, I tried to reflect
on the delays of my feelings:
So afraid of them and women,
they said, *unheroic at table,*
just feeling sorry for yourself.

You want to know what I think?
Instead of spiraling thoughts
about what I once had thought,
I may retire, muddled, misled,
return to emotions displayed,

as mundane as when I read
The Poky Little Puppy as a kid:
Little Poky, help yourself
to diminish your story like
the poky little mess you are...

Now, will I live on the streets
because of these facts? Perhaps
I'm not the kind who can save
my childhood with a smith's
most striking characteristics:

Little missive, your mystery's
one who chooses sadder songs
has chosen to sing through me...
I throw up some dirt to see
what might happen, or not—

but, isn't it dangerous
to run red lights, committed
to how I should be taken
off the streets? Not even close,
I'm at less than zero when

my latest mistakes form lakes
that were never shining so
long ago as now with what's
left to haunt me here inside
this fuzzy body infinitely,

past park railings, leaf debris.

DAWDLING

1.

Today, with scents of soil on a first warm breeze,
you perceive a whole new philosophy in
just hanging out, reading some old notes fallen
from pockets of your pocket dictionary:
"By now, you're in no position to maintain
your abnormal narrowing breadth, becoming
like somebody else, with less and less to know."

Assuming you will always wake to utter
confusions of demands, content to go on
lying on the grass, speaking ill of the dead,
not joining in songs of sadness for ghosts within
the limits of their hushed museums, you still don't
regret how you've always sought greater solace
when met with less impressive schools of thought.

2.

You, who often felt way in over your head,
are still trying to tell how you got hung up;
yet, you've already found new ways to get by:
by the skin of your teeth. You watch the others:
when your carton drops, a dozen eggs will crack,
all the yolks run out– but nothing of theirs breaks–
while you always leave behind some telltale tracks.

Not for the first time, nor will it be your last,
you feel like some victim, surviving a storm
of seeing entire collections of the culture
of tall smokestacks spewing, spent, amid stark lines
of new cars, bright sun shining down on them—
till these scenes only seem like things torn apart
from heady days of living beyond your means.

3.

With questions still turning in useless circles,
you ask yourself how you might ever complete
your self-becoming– like a work-in-progress
for anyone who, wanting to live within
another world by standing up to the old
theories of fallen mankind, wonders, "If this
is my job, why not just keep on doing it?"

You spent so much time in light activities,
constantly diving into the sun and sea
to get a good tan, an even brighter smile,
you thought you could make yourself still lighter,
eventually find some unmasked glory in the sky—
yet, when you recall those names you called the dead,
your thoughts will begin to fill your eyes with tears.

4.

These tragic feelings seem opposed to reason:
the boy is taken in by arthritic hands that say,
"These are mine, but they will be *your* hands someday—"
and though the young girl's neck isn't yet broken,
pictures of her dead body lie trembling within
those places where "Life may give you a reduced
sentence," they say, "but you'll never be released."

Learning some new roles in rose-colored stages,
you imagine you've seen some things no one else
might see, desires playing out in you as new
surprises— but you're not so surprised by those
low suns hurtling toward you at dawn, leaving you
alone again for many nights, old instincts
intact within the soft moist hands of childhood.

5.

Many have inherited these warring genes,
it seems, but you've kept yours to yourself for years,
turning down the swords, the brandishing of steel,
for your own intangible reasons. By now,
the several wars you've faced don't even feel real—
with hate's insinuating voice, for instance,
lying right inside you, yet listlessly, still.

When you walk into the full-blown tornado
to reach the intractable heart, controlling
your difficulties with difficulty, with a new
correspondence to how bad things used to be,
perhaps you'd be happier among palm fronds
as the sunset slides away from you off-shore
and the lights go on above, across those skies...

6.

As fires return to the hands that started them,
fire becomes like any other anxious word
to save for the occasions when you'd savor
somebody falling in love with someone else,
two sensibilities meeting, then dealing
with their unpacking of baggage, setting up
some new detours inside of their darkness.

As you're steering through a space you never knew
into parts unknown, transforming your gestures
from a letting go of them into your past,
after putting up with those sad facts, you'd sort
yourself out– but, before you can do away
with greasiness spreading on these days in waves,
the waves become softer, like love-battered hearts.

7.

Now, everyone's getting ready again for
the advent of summer, the summit, putting out
new questions like soft feelers into gardens,
so that the eyes of very deep blue that wax
against other people's bodies come to seem
less dangerous, even unremarkable,
like anything else that rests, or rots, within.

As you come back down by way of rocky slopes,
the stones' sounds, answering, seem the only sense
that might survive. In this case, they overlap
with your own internal maps: as certain as
the stopped clock, the hairbrush, with fallen hair in
the basin– found, like your memories of that place
where you dug up some old bones once, descending.

OUR BODIES, OURSELVES

Hounded by gibes, we come to our bodies
by their secret looks, like heavy sentinels
that keep hanging around us, hanging out
about the house, still keeping the subtle
demeanors of contrarian commentators.

We think we made the mistakes we made
when all of our past sensual capacities
were still comparatively strong; but now,
when we meet, come together meat to meat,
out of our clothes, we feel completely wrong.

We only wear such masks, we think, if we
feel in desperate need of some covering–
but we'll be taking new physicals soon,
with possible new embarrassments for
things we'll never want to mention again.

Most of the time we don't like our curt flesh,
shadowy lines flung onto hardwood floors–
yet, there's still our own decision to level
the ugly facts: statistics say we'll wind up
far from happy, or sad, far away from home.

OUR FUTURE TENSE

If that time feels overdue,
yet overdone for us to see
in these noisy restaurants
the two of us questioning
our new plan for penance
so that we would proceed
in our mutual recognition
of such tense negotiations,

to all intents and purposes,
seeing to the end of a nose
while looking for our souls
seems about the same thing:
reports from the recordings
of our childhoods long ago,
making the same mistakes
we usually made back then.

We'll never forget the styles
we wore, weaving our trails
into some futures, but keep
to inaction right about now
because it's all about those
who lie waiting for the light,
the light to change, we think,
to show which ways to turn.

Are there no deeper shadows
on this land than two beings'

lost inside our acts? If we see
bone or marrow in our tracks,
will it mean we must be more
careful in this yearning state:
how we will have to improve,
we believe, what we believe?

CONSERVATION OF ENERGY

A man falls fast asleep,
and soon he dreams,
but when he does,
he mills and churns
as if his thoughts
would never stop
their old commotions:
A poem always keeps
its shape, he thinks,
as opposed to prose.

That's his problem,
as he watches words
fly down corridors,
words like animals
not yet quite feral
but still living under
the eyes of their god
who releases them
from velvet cages
to kill men and die.

Fresh corpses grow
along those roads,
but new generations
might never know
what ruined castles
were like before
they began to play

violent childhood
games in them– and
as you may know,

I am that man.

II.

COSTUMES

*"As you define me
as a human being,
expect me to act
exactly like one."*

PROPOSAL

Open your eyes:
if you see a bird,
you too might fly,

use intelligence
to find your place
in the universe,

granting that you
keep suffocating
families, with all

their imaginary
hook-lines, sinkers,
under control in

clown-size type shoes
down here below.

PATIENT

With a psychoanalyst, you tried to make
some sense of the lives you'd actually led,
rather than ones for which you'd yearned
  while trying to earn some parental pity,
approbation, in places that once seemed
so important to your growing up: houses
cold or burning, bitter towns torn down.

Living within the narrowed freedoms of
desperate cities, why did so many have
  noses smudged, rubbed in filthy poses?
You hated the blithe innocence of those
looking good for the sake of the familiar
family mirage, that sustenance of blood
in which you hardly recognized your own.

Bountifully covered with scars, in a long
cutting embrace, you looked away before
  crossing to tentative cures, flying away
for awhile to some safer space where you
wished to be ensconced, spirited beyond
with all those other careening survivors
of parents' stony silence, blandishments.

You tried to make a statement in your skin
as you carefully worked that long way back
down from the head to the heart: you'd heal
  if they'd yield; or, they'd heal if you yielded;
and so on and so forth, till your time was up...
They drove you there and hung around until
you came out; then they drove you back again.

PRODIGAL

Prodigal, like the bad son who became
a favored brother, you left home to find
a father, so late, looking for some sign
another father might have given him.
Holding to the spirits you grew up with,
understood, you tried to live another life,
an old ideal increasing toward that end:
Isn't it true dead stars turned into men?

Without quite knowing how brutal rules
of revelations worked– like an antidote
to telling truths beyond whisperings of
a gods' justice, judgments based on faith–
feeling relieved of what was in your hands,
the multicolored coat-tails you stepped on
broken off like limbs, you felt sadder when
some spirit creature wouldn't be your guide.

You couldn't say what kinds of wild animals
still wallowed like hippos along that Nile,
that Euphrates, but with a chastened smile
returned to other kinds of beasts instead.
You ordered the pain above constant floods
of disappointments, seeing how such griefs
refracted things: unanswerable, the way
waves' sounds take time to reach far shores...

While you were still the bodily embodiment
of some anonymous sites within this world,

your occupation was to hoard such scenes:
you felt held in a cage, where, aloft in flight,
within a sunny meadow once seen through
clear windows shimmering in rising heat,
removed, running from your own reflections,
you saw how far away everything seemed.

GEIGER COUNTERS

You recently saw one of the loves of your life
changed beyond all former easy recognition,
having turned into an older version of herself,
with crepe-neck and wrinkled lips as symptoms.

It reminded you of when you were quite young
and your father took the whole family on outings
to Bear Mountain State Park to hunt for uranium,
waving shiny metal cylinders around in cold air.

As you tramped through muck, waiting for clicks,
beyond occasional noisy background radiations,
you always came up empty in the course of days
spent searching up and down those cold slopes.

It was like your latest search for love these days:
waving that phallic wand, receiving glimmers
of mutual interests in a difficult environment,
interest never adding up to much of anything.

And was that your father's intention in the end,
just to trudge up and down the potential paths
as an exercise for its own sake? Was it enough,
even if nothing was found at the heart, in fact,

to wait for significant radiation to register in
a series of clicks, a charged atmosphere, then?
After a lifetime of such exposure to those rays
from the nuclear equipment his company made,

he died from leukemia before his natural term,
like the other young men who worked with him,
sickened and dying long before his expectation.
Or maybe it was just from his strenuous affairs.

TURNED IN TO THE AUTHORITIES

It was long ago, and yet, too late, when I first saw
how little losses are confined to the here and now;
yet, the way things would always remain the same.
I lived alone in an actual house, on my own plane:
as some others made their many messes each day,
"I can't wait to clean up my own bad acts," I'd say,
regarding all my stalling as a form of slow torture
as my former bad relations snored in the corners.

Would anyone else bide nights with me?, I'd ask,
who never took whatever was left, it seemed, of
others' good advice. My proposition was to track
the carcasses on canvasses, despite admonitions
to chuck it all into the kitchen sink– until I chose
to throw everything out in the gutter: table scraps,
weeks-old foot-long hot dogs, the used kitty-litter
filled with cat- scratch fevers, back into the trash.

Closer to a deadline, there was much left to pay for,
with old, as-yet-undisclosed, large amounts of cash.
At the summer solstice some darkness still crept in:
my evenings seemed beyond reach of such steamy
afternoons' more vigorous debates. Feeling freed
of overhanging clouds, falling between the cracks,
I felt thirsty as some tree's hollow limbs, to perhaps
drag myself back to some sort of normalcy someday.

I claimed no control over the time's new brutality,
or how it might look when cops just happened by

and I'd start passing through the outer barricades,
confronting long corridors under a different name...
I'm getting ready for yet another court appearance,
a crowd's crush, amphitheater's hum, steep tariffs
in due course– with all of those old police citations
remaining still at home, either unopened or unpaid.

THE MESSENGER

One day, a friend sent you *The Messenger*.
Returning to your former childhood home,
a place you thought would always stay the same,
you found one tree, your name inscribed, still there.
With darkness falling, touched by what you'd seen
of greenness growing into blue grass sighing
across those fields, you walked, remembering,
feeling further back, between *now* and *then*.

You never thought that you'd come home to this
old yearning– a consequence of past sins
drawn like bold tattoos all over your skin,
which couldn't contain a spreading sickness:
you'd come to know how you were misconceived,
how a father would beat his bastard child…
There was a bank across the river, which, wild,
you robbed; then turned yourself in, almost relieved.

Once inside their Missouri River prison
that hovered near the fault line, New Madrid,
like your friend, you felt that everything you did
just kept more awful things from happening:
how your soul filled your breath and made your hand
to use that force with which you'd almost kill
someone– which made you want to kill them all,
and still created death, intransigence in Man.

With yellow-fingered stains inside your brain
from celled experiments, you knew you lacked

what you'd once gathered: light like laser shafts,
a light by which to catch some sight of heaven.
You'd been too crazy once, running around
from one fix to the next, to ever try to plan
for this uncorrected world; but, calmer then,
you swallowed fateful capsules, settled down.

FROM CINCINNATI

From a distance, with its upright attitudes,
it seems merely a pastiche of earnest German
interpretations of life's taller buildings
stretching under cloud parades from other skies
all passing by, these streets rarely leading out
to those cities of your dreams you lost touch with
long ago– the shifts of fashion, the daily
gossip, the names of who and what were *in*...

By now, you no longer think much useful truth
resides in such nostalgia, still languishing in
another country where *what's happening* means
something else entirely, torturing your sleep.
Yet, this comfy little enclave you'd call home
serves you well, and you like working within
its provincial systems, without memories
of all those former ongoing bankruptcies...

One day, freaking out over some minor
money matter that was bound to burst loose
sooner or later, getting ready to dash over
to the bank manager's on your mid-day break,
in the assumption of such errands, could you
consider how much heavy breathing betrayed
the significance of the event? There were
probably no answers to your presumptions

of others' criminal transgressions after
never keeping records for so many years,

but, other than terminal guilt, nothing fit
your poverty-stricken thoughts more than this:
with fears of debts running wilder the closer
you came to your house, soon you'd be breaking
into piggy banks, taking them down without
any constraint, withdrawing all your funds.

AFTER THE BREAK-IN

From where an agile burglar climbed in through
a low broken window, your living room
targeted, sacked; as cops begin dusting
doorknobs for fingerprints, gathering up
the glitter there; in complicity with
the walls surrounding you, you soon feel freed
of all previous illusions as you
fill out police reports, insurance forms,
at the dead center of your life's bulls-eye.

If you need to drink more now in order
to stay in touch with some sense of former
privacy, to these sad activities
you've added the burdens of mixing in
some recent reinterpretations of
overseeing your invaded family's care:
for all your complaints about your hard luck,
you'd still rather keep your head in the clouds,
because you know no better solution.

You'll have no money left over because,
once they send insurance cancellations,
you know how all your wages will be spent.
Pacing within that fragile, emptied shell,
you mull over losses for days, content
to retrace deeper waves of discontent
as bright lights bounce off the chandeliers,
alluring, assuring that you'll never
let anyone, or anything, in again.

ANTISOCIAL

If I'm antisocial, I can't bend,
you say, *the world to my will,*

lying vigilant in the darkness,
seeking some new particulars

in those undersides of parked
cars along their busy avenues,

with remnants of late summer
storms in filthy pools of water

stinking in the crease between
the sidewalks and the asphalt,

where a sheet of metal covers
the holes for ditches they dug

six feet deep beneath a street,
which masses of people sweat

under covers in fear to behold.

ON THE SPECTRUM

If, when we first meet you, you make a slight bow
or curtsy for curt moments, we may see how,
because you've so rarely been taken up in
any other's hands, it won't disappoint you
if we seem not to notice how much private pain,
with little else at your command, flows in,
usually, against almost everyone's
ominously oblivious observations.

Although you've always had so little to say
about the conditions to which you're subject,
struggling with words, machine- or heartbeat-piqued,
a language with which you may never connect
at intersections of our ways of being,
sometimes you might try to give us back something
in courageous exchange. But it may seem strange,

like a box inside a box, wrapped up, intact–
or just another miscommunication
quite easily ignored... Yet, if all those plain
coatings of fears of others are to protect
your own begrudging of a trying to please,
you only seem harder to deal with because
you'll always have the energy to maintain
these continuous superficialities.

APOSTATE

Bound to be bound by their pioneers,
implacable, dead, you expose yourself
to spirits in space at their gatherings,

as if you'd chosen airborne contagion
in your desire to be infected by gods.
You'd aspired to be that unplacatable–

yet everyone yells, until you can't tell
who you are, aren't, or even where, till
you see an image of a golden doorknob

out of there to where you breathe again
in suddenly cleansed, re-freshened air.

UNDERGROUND

Those were the people you were willing to sell,
but that got you put on that gravy train to hell:
arrived, you saw what you had never conceived,
and began to do your own slow writhing dance.
With everyone dead alive there, supernaturally,
you knew you'd met your last, eternal audience.

All these examples of flesh offered up samples
of bloodlines you read in past heroic struggles--
but what you shared as you dropped down there
were unrenewed ambitions, discarded gestures,
while the bodies seemed like old torn costumes
no matter which ways they ever had worn them.

The thoughts scribbled in patterns, impervious,
were marking the madness in lines and surfaces
of those who don't have any chance left to wake
from all their forerunners' farthest future fears;
who'd tremble and shake at first great mistakes,
as their sobbing makes cruel music to your ears.

III.

DARK MATTERS

"God made everything out of nothing;
that nothingness still shows through."
—Paul Valéry

INVOCATION

If you're with me for the rest of my days,
I won't need, you say, *all kinds of deeds*
to make compassionate comparisons,
generously spreading your open maw
with a big black patch of hair that splays.

It's a communion in which you've done
great things for me– or a great deal of harm;
for you've always been my secret lover,
as if you cured Job better than he knew;
or maybe, with him, you just had more fun.

I think I act the ways I do because
I thought I deserved love when it wasn't
a scandal shared. O, Love, in your domain,
what should I do? I'm a small thing to you,
as I am to my enemies, I suppose.

Yet, if I can divert your attention
from left out to right now, my confession
will be determined by how you listen
to my words, breathing in, deeply breathing
out all that I've done, what I won't mention.

Though you and no one else knows of a shore
to which I might be afterward removed,
we're partners, too, even when my ideals
are *man's* ideas of what's in your dark touch
in moments of making literature.

For now, practically speaking, I'm sure
enough by myself, learning how to love
by knowing what I'll have to pay to live,
to endure. And it's a joy not to have
to believe in any other god anymore.

PROVOCATIONS OF THE MASTER OF ICE

I dreamt I dreamt about him in the world,
which represents him as an oracle of ruin,
monstrous, unanswerable, misunderstood,
as he increased the scale of movements in
the raging tides and said,

'My wintry storms won't keep you warm.'
As he grew in his powers over his people
every day in every way– to be recollected
only in some false reports of his activities
from early childhood on–

this leader, who always had nerve enough
to mislead us, willed himself away before
settling into his head without the betrayal
of immense and arcane ways, covering up,
making everything worse.

*

After millennia of rage for broken words,
all his many public taunts about our lives,
we weren't saved from his voice, or body,
that dangerous garment to be swept up in.

Groups of neighbors, we knew, took few
or no risks; yet, those followers often felt
his acid confrontations; for anything less
would be grist for more amoral activities.

Insuring his own safety as he tried to kill
a few million more people along the way,
we were most fearful of how deep he was
into killing, with lives passing quickly by.

*

Some said it's a crock as he came to wrap
our buildings in his dark talk: he'd folded
himself in a flag, it's true, rustling sounds
briefly overheard; slowly and surely, then,
        forcing new perspectives:

for all that congregations heard from him,
he'd show no moderation in word or work,
discreetly rebuffing all his followers when
turning his cheek, unblocking frozen seas,
        speaking down to us thus,

'You love the world's face, but not its soul;
and so you've fallen out of favor with me.
Yet, I'll let you reverse things, at my ease,
since you wish to leave the earth after all,'
        hanging in a crooked tree.

*

He didn't feel like walking on the waters,
but, beautifully becalmed, lay on a beach,
leaving this world he'd disappeared from
one day, within a passing floating bubble.

He still seemed ten feet tall, in no danger
from famished fools trying to fill the void:
for every heavy man sinking into a wave,
he'd find another as reckless for that task.

Yet, when we pulled him from his hidden
un-defiled secret place, filling with a past
that wasn't and the past that was, he said,
'I give you my blessing, instead of a curse.'

MISLABELED, RECLASSIFIED, CONTINUING

I hear some rumblings in the sky
of lost faith, whose mourners, after all,
live and abide inside a seemingly
serious breach of their security,
the housebreakers already vanished.

With revelations of gods looking down
with testimonies from their high views
of a world emptied again of their works,
my neighbors continue their conversations
with policemen writing summonses.

With the impatience of gods, they may think
I'm merely like some lost lord of my life,
speaking the only words of praise they have
for what I am: "Here's a man who has loved
with only the weight of his motives."

But I know that's just another story
without any consistent argument,
and I, too, may soon be feeling foolish,
abolished, because this world holds many
things, but never hangs onto them itself.

While I've seen it's best not to organize
my hormones to converge on some others
now and again, to marry better next time,
since these kinds of mystic misalliance
are like scratching chalk on a blackboard,

I think that, helplessly, I'll change back
to a piece of chalk, changing all the locks
on the doors to where I seem meant to be,
my big news gone wrong; yet, still inside me,
a pride that hurts, burning deeper than coal.

FIRST CIRCUIT

In a circuit of a burnt woods,
as I was vehemently exploring,
opening a newly violated space,

it wasn't only my recognition of
what flora had been there before
I circled bare, scorched, Goliaths:

when I felt some childhood waters
roiling inside me, intertwined with
the sky catching moonlight beyond,

the planets circling, pulling me taut,
showed cold faces to faces on earth,
upon the earth as it is in the heavens.

NEW NEWS OF THE UNIVERSE

Discovering how, after much time
folding fields of "space-time," like
cosmic origami, into some original
argument for how things need to be,

the new news of the universe creates
incomprehensible designs, entangled
bits of matter converging on sublime
new folds upon folds inside my mind.

Communicating across 'empty' space
how forces work with indeterminacy
beyond us, our finite understanding
of *no agency* only makes this worse

because, we're merely local eddies
in the chaotic mind of the universe.

DARK MATTERS

In the gap between *Why* and *Why not,*
congregations sit with their recordings
reporting what they believe: "Why not?"

If we fight how, even now as we play it,
their game we don't believe in deceives,
the final results are *always* guaranteed.

As a faith in miracles would be a creed
through which they're less likely to see
a material darkness filling the universe,

we could be their bitten victims in pain
their vicious dogs may try to bite again,
because we'll never beg, but only bleed.

A VIRTUAL ENCYCLOPEDIA

The ex-minister who lived down the lane,
propounding with such high authority
a curse on everything coursing strongly
through evanescent veins, one day was gone.

From too many boring formal inquiries
into why we loved our trivial *things*,
that noble speaker had speaker's fatigue
about our souls' lost possibilities.

Pious plans that his people used to share
showed off *his* intelligence as he contrived
directories for our slowly-dying lives,
the numbers not adding up anymore.

We were staving off his heavens with dread
before he left, putting on his sternest face,
and didn't want to light the candle flames
in which we'd be conceived as living dead.

*

For days after, in mourning haze we bore,
we saved ourselves from what we might become
if he ever came back– for, all that time,
the years' disparities rubbed our nerves raw.

Reflecting on our good and bad qualities,
we felt oppressed, of course, as, formerly
hopeful, we were annoyed and unhappy
about not indulging our identities.

Yet, on good days, it was better to know
how we might still split our shadows– except
for those holy ones who'd be like bad guests,
each head placed onto their necks like ghosts.

Trying to remain hopeful as we dropped
toward our new goals was to be excited
by dangers, to which we were addicted–
but it wasn't long before we had to stop.

*

We pursued resumes, but couldn't keep
our shy adventurous soft warm bodies,
our attributes, our personalities,
within these encyclopedic needs:

"In flesh," we felt, "surely there were, or are
some salient shadows left–" transferring warm
ideas inside our own tightly knit palms
to encyclopedias of virtual charms...

We'd start over again, awaiting berths
in pews by thick wooden doors. When we'd leave
those confessionals, we'd say, "Step aside, please–"
our every step down steps into turned earth.

Dark velour filled our green exteriors,
with setting suns always parting behind
a wrinkled tarp backdrop, pink-mauve beyond,
painting our meanings the rubble of years.

HOMAGE TO LUCIA

With your real-life escapes from the ER,
or other dangerous places too numerous
by now to mention, without any breaks
from a long-suffering, long suffered life,

as your days dwindle, we see you above
the mercy of others without any regrets,
unveiling your lost cheer-leading youth,
a whole body left from what lies within.

But what's that angry red mark crawling
down the middle of your back when you
undress to confess the pain in a series of
social situations, each requiring the cane?

Arriving at soles at the bottoms of shoes,
you'd never want to make an earlier exit
from the party's parting fun, your funeral,
who'd never wish to get into a coffin alone.

A SHIP IN PORT

Accepting what you thought,
that everyone you found there
was scum, you determined that
all the respectable world
was merely an illusion,
and lived accordingly
to an angry old age:

"To live, and then let die."
As you thought everyone had
his own decisions to make,
you wanted to levitate
a cold-blooded woman.

Made with the thick ham
of your good right arm,
the syntax of the sentence
you wrote: "You look like
some stationary machine,
standing there," but didn't
get to ride her till the end...

Your children are likely
to learn many new things
beyond your life's knowledge,
things now rusting slowly
back into the earth and sea.

OUTSIDE PHOENIX

Blindfolded, beside a ravine,
cold winds within a darkness
beating into wet open wounds,

a people gathering, sucking up
so much of their virtual worlds
they find inside this unreal one,

these dying wander into craters,
eaten forever in stadiums full of
dust and weapons creating death

on this earth: whatever wretched
prayer they place to placate them,
halfway hesitant, bright, halftone,

they'll always have their religions,
until it's just them crawling home
in a daze, into some farther room.

ENGRAVED

When we were feeling well,
walking about by ourselves,
"Let's do it soon," you said,
"tell the words that we read
on stones to other people:
'The most affectionate days
of their lives,' for example."

Did mourners deserve this
quiet quest for old relations
unearthed from their tombs?
We were still notorious then
for our great perseverance,
and said, "Aren't we getting
much better at this digging?"

There was a crying of dogs
as we dug, as we bent down
or stood still in fullest view,
till a black car almost hit us.
We found a rabbit and mole
huddled in a burrowed hole,
a small cache of buried coins.

The old world felt new again
as we eyed their graven lines.
And when it was all dug up,
all dug up, we'd go to show
the world what we had seen.

IV.

STAGES

Content:
Continent,
Competent,
Confident,
Independent.

Discontent:
Dependent,
Repentant,
Incontinent,
Incompetent.

The End.

I USED TO TRY TO KEEP A DISTANCE

but since I've come a long way since,
my inclination is to stare down death,
to fight it at the entrance to my house,
for I don't want others to see the time
getting shorter in my one and only life.

While notoriety isn't what I like to hear
about every day, in a big city the whole
landscape consists only of other people:
in its labyrinths we each make our own
contribution to the pathway unwinding.

"Never dare to eat low berries," they say,
"they may be poisonous." I want to speak
so no one may take offense at what I say,
as I've learned to stop talking about how
there's some salvation in the unraveling.

I'm ready to write with ruled paper now
instead of blank. I often made things up
to fill in those incomprehensible blanks:
"It doesn't matter where you are, Death
gets its hold on you, wherever you hide."

With time becoming like a pulse inside,
how should I feel? *As if you never knew
that I was yours, or that you were mine,
we've lived each others' life,* says Death
to me on the streets of my city each day.

SOME CALL IT SLEEP

Now whenever you see
the men or women who
blame personal failures
on their current *milieux*,

condemning themselves
like indicted politicians
who make protestations
of their total innocence,

such sad self-deception
no longer seems so bad:
losing your old mother,
you'd adore a dead dad;

you'll also lie, too soon,
within a grave violence
that comes to all before
the sleep before silence.

SONG FOR A NEW OLD AGE

"You can't always get what you want—
but sometimes you get what you need."
—The Rolling Stones

If you wanted perfection, by now you've learned
it's just something that you're never going to get.
Since you've been troubled, and still feel burned,
you might go on well enough with less to expect.

Revising all reminders of former athletic being,
you no longer expect your legs to be formidable;
nor are you sad at thoughts of the others' seeing
a grandfatherly type with an empty water bottle.

But if that's not enough, there still are questions
of changing a machine's setting down to *Vibrate,*
not accepting for life these inhumane conditions,
until you're driven home from the gym in a rage.

Since your present can't hold your former place,
learning the legitimacy of new losses about you
in the slow dissolution of each previous lost age,
no one can help you and you don't want them to.

Yet, you might feel proud of how you've gone on
campaigning for the pasts inside of you to sleep:
soon, you'll be patiently dancing, up and down,
letting go of your pasts, for awhile, or for keeps.

ON THE WARD

You once were pleased to be able to think
your flesh in hospitals could be critiqued,
computing myriad scripts, as you went,
of some good hand guiding an instrument.

Like so many other cancer patients there,
you consider your sickness second-nature,
but you can't quite connect to how it looks
amid the speculations about how it works.

"The roots of tumors come from the blood;
did you think cysts would end in such mud?"
You dream they say such stuff as you sleep,
some last call to find how your body weeps.

Whatever else, they have their monopolies
on your X-rays, those illuminated beasts,
like sheltered carcasses that, too, may fall
like fresh flesh into freezers down the hall.

In the exploration below something-below
of what dictates your cancer's quiet growth,
now, if they see you going, too fast, or slow,
will they cut back on their giving of chemo?

With less inhibition as you grow more sick,
recalling freed up days that you'd commit
to happiness, on that inland bed's life-raft,
your body fills, a glass of water in the glass.

LATE RITES

At the door of nothing in particular
each night, you choose between the abyss
and your bed, expecting nothing less
than blood bubbling like carbonated water.

Like anyone whose heart still spasms,
deeply distressed by each odd contraction,
lungs straining, blood pumping in dysfunction,
your riddled chest filled with embolisms,

unwilling the death of yourself alone
but sick enough to leave this world behind,
you'll stay alive until your time to die:

with unwarranted shrugs, you'll just go on
breaking things up, breaking things down–
a whole lot of moves toward a hole in the ground.

OUR MOTHER

1.

She counted on conformity
to everydayness in her days,
but never found a better way
to try to save herself; or else,
she wouldn't be assuaged by
her forcing us to be with her
for mostly mundane matters,
wishing for some better way
to relinquish her life instead.

By then, in cloaking honesty,
wrapped in etiquettes anew,
she wouldn't be the only one
who didn't delve so deep into
a fate that can't be improved
by medical systems, separate
from death in digital displays
in which her terminal disease
spread quickly down a queue.

2.

Was she afraid of pain
lying too deeply within,
or tears' endless oceans
surrounding everything?

Exposing new emnities
with a rueful regularity,
barely recovering from
a brutality she inflicted

on herself and everyone,
if she ever began to cry,
our mother used to sigh,
My tears may never end.

3.

Will I be with my mother at the end,
or walking around elsewhere, alone?
I don't know– whatever seems best
for a simulation of 'good family ties.'

How many others will it take to give
the attention or credence she craves
before she'll relax, in or out of coma,
an almost inexhaustible will entirely?

Warning those visitors who seem so
unfamiliar with her indomitable ego,
I'd say, *She likes fiction* and *friction,
but the hardest part's still left: to go.*

And when this dying process is over,
let it be said, *Soon, we'll finally feel
released from the incalculable pain,
when she'll finally be, entirely, gone.*

DREAMING OF FREEDOM

"You doubt I have a tear inside my chest,
  right here above my heart, I guess, where
my breast used to be. I'm unlucky that way,"

you say. So, yes, it's hard; but doesn't have
to be any harder than this. And as the sun
comes up before us sitting there, I want to

protect you in advance, to see if, when you
return, it might touch you to hear me say
  that you're not so very different from me...

As we were urging new worlds to emerge,
as if the world was reduced to some facts,
which were becoming like our future lists

for those who wanted their happy endings
to adventures for some adventurers' sakes.
for the duration of our mournful memories,

now I want you to pull your bandages away,
because that's what I've always wanted to do.

NOTES FOR A FAREWELL

She often seemed a cool observer
of this cold world, awakening
on snow-bound mornings wondering
if there were far worse fates for her
in store, or just some darker skies.
It was the way that she said *No*,
while many others weren't so
convincingly unsatisfied.

An understudy dressing up
each night for a possible role,
her grieving face was prone to call
attention to itself, a prop
she kept inside a darkened room,
an indication of her problems
achieving any new distinctions
beyond dim hopes of ending soon.

Arriving at some stillness, lying
before iced spectacles long past
the winter solstice, could she ask
for more, beyond identifying
a hanging thread, things left behind?
She'd breathe in deeply as she could
an air of leaving things for good,
still ill-prepared for such ill wind…

Unchanged, what could she ever do
to stop or blunt the latest night's

invasions of her morbid thoughts
or question what she'd sink into?
Could there be any better finish,
as meaningless as flesh kept safe
by her convenient disbelief
in capacities diminished?

In days that marked her, she was back
to thinking what to do with shadows
moving toward her dimming windows,
projecting death, while hinting at
a comprehensive understanding
of future relaxations, ending
in half-forgotten self-forgetting,
the letting go of everything.

AFTER THE BELOVED SUICIDES

What makes some people so desperate to try
to leave the world? We can't make them stay
whenever they say that they deserve to die.

As morning turns to night, we think it's right
to want to tell our own truths when we learn,
not as hot nor cold like them, how they tried:

"I'm not going, yet; don't look for me there."
But, not long after, they cash in their chips—
some ending in the ground, some in the air.

Left behind, the rest of us study here, alone,
the terse words they'd spoken all that time:
a fine dust left in their tracks, they are gone.

Fearing all those implicit, intrepid passions
for hooks on their walls, we can't turn away
from nooses they set. "We have our reasons
to leave," we say, yet wish to continue to stay.

LITTLE STONE HOUSE

Jon Anderson, 1940-2007

Burnt orange, lime green walls
with high yellow ceilings in
the Tuscan house in Tucson,

white clouds passing over
in soft safe puffs, where you
projected disappointments

on a world that continued
its patient process, before
you blew up your garage;

then you ran for your life,
past each saguaro cactus
on which you placed a faith,

your robe hanging open
without a hood, over burnt
remains beyond the fence...

After last year's bad drought,
your clothing drying mid-air
when tossed, past lilac fields,

you knew what you wanted:
if your friends wouldn't be
saved you couldn't be either.

Your answer was that part
of your art was lost, far out
beyond those hidden stars,

approaching the unknown
ends of everything.

AFTER THAT

When the famous poet at last had died,
starting with a single stroke, his secrets
arrived like assignations in our heads,
opening us to all that dark inside.

Like organelles, his words guided us
to elucidate each created thought
with delicacy; wherever he'd gone,
we'd go on spreading lines out from there:

"Your eyes will be with us until we die."
But then, at a distance, inside the nights,
we dreamed the days' doings of our lovers,
who dreamed about some other points of light.

And thus, we discovered a universe
of our own creations, with everyone
speaking out their own small truths as if
each poet's name became only their brand.

Or was there never any new universe
for us to know, as we used our own senses
to come into some greater maturities
by small steps, taking no trips without them?

If we couldn't bear his previous names
for our lives, our object then was to strive
for freedom to sift our future restrictions
from all those expedient possibilities.

We'd made a mess of things, apparently,
importantly so: in one sense, we'd fallen
under his representations; but, after that,
everything else seemed gloriously freed.

CEMETERY CEREMONY

A summer day gorgeously swimming
in sunshine outrageously glimmering
isn't mine, but just a duty to feel grim,
even guilty, hearing the music in flags
flapping, swelling, half-mast on poles,
like quelled messages that won't stop
playing over and over inside myself.

Reawakening to this world, reacting
like a child to these earthen smells,
takes me back, fast: in some prior
emergencies, ignorance prescribed
the only name I'd think to call first—
but now, her old pictures on display,
my feelings seem bound up inside
the breaking of bonds between us.

If I cry more easily now than I ever
was seen to before, I never worshiped
this fallen world's creation, but weigh
it out again with new pangs I'll suffer:
feeling foolish at a last service absorbed
by sunlight, I find myself still crying out
to create a better world inside my head.

JOHN IS GONE

and the world will be
a little emptier place
without him for me.

i.m., John Ashbery

NOTES

This book is dedicated to my late parents, and my late and living friends — especially Judith Larsen.

P. 11: *The Poky Little Puppy* is a book for children, about an always-tardy dog who came home too late to eat his supper, so missed his chocolate pudding dessert.

P. 53: 'no agency' refers to 'information' sent between 'entangled' subatomic particles that act and react in tandem instantaneously, without any intermediary, across 'empty' space– unlike the 'causes and effects' in our macroscopic world, where, in "the butterfly effect," something as small as the flapping of a butterfly's wings might ultimately help cause the formation of a typhoon somewhere else on earth.

P. 57: *Lucia* is Lucia Perillo, poet, born in 1958, diagnosed with MS 1988, died in 2016.

All unattributed quotations in the text are by the author.

About the Author
DAVID SCHLOSS

He was born in Brooklyn, New York, in 1944, and educated at Columbia University, The University of Southern California Cinema School, Brooklyn College (BA), and The Iowa Writers Workshop (MFA). He taught at the University of Cincinnati and Miami University (Ohio) from which he retired as Emeritus Professor of English in December, 2014.

He has published five full-length poetry collections: *The Beloved* (Ashland Poetry Press, 1973), *Sex Lives of the Poor and Obscure*, (Carnegie Mellon University Press, 2001), *Group Portrait from Hell* (Carnegie Mellon University Press, 2009), *Reports from Babylon and Beyond* (Dos Madres Press), 2015), *The Heartbeat as an Ancient Instrument* (Dos Madres Press, 2020; plus three chapbooks, *Legends* (The Windmill Press, 1976), *Greatest Hits* (Pudding House Press, 2004), *Behind the Eyes* (Dos Madres Press 2005), as well as scores of poems in literary journals and anthologies over the years.

www.ingramcontent.com/pod-product-compliance
Lightning Source LLC
Chambersburg PA
CBHW051224120626
46547CB00013B/1503